Did You Know?

Did you know that your subconscious mind is programmed to find whatever it is you have lost? So losing weight is something one can do, but the subconscious mind will actually look for its safe return because that is its job! So, what can you do about this? Releasing weight is a whole other game plan that actually works long term. That is what this book is all about. By learning why the weight is there to begin with, we are free to release it. Once we let it go, we are able to achieve the health, weight and body image we desire.

Miranda Sullivan

Before she knew how to "Say YES"

And After!

Disclaimer

This book / workbook is intended for informational purpose only, it in itself is not a guarantee of success.   If there are any medical considerations regarding your health and weight, consulting your Doctor before making any changes is advised. Please take care of your body, it is the only one you've got.

The Dedication

To all who have ever struggled, worried, fixated, suffered, been angry, felt inadequate, unattractive, undesired, frustrated and otherwise just plain unhappy about where they find themselves regarding their weight, body image and or appearance. We understand what it means to avoid mirrors and to pretend that it just doesn't matter.

It does matter however because YOU matter.

We offer these pages as an answer, a path, a process and or a philosophy that we sincerely wish will be a life changing, inspiring, enlightening and empowering experience for you. We want you to know that you are not alone and that there is always hope with every new moment. As the saying goes; live, love, laugh and from this moment on remember, you do deserve your dreams. Thank you for allowing us this time with you.

A Special Thanks to everyone who assisted us every step of the way. To our fearless editor, Kim for his diligent eyes and loving heart. To our partner and friend Massood for his creativity, love and patience. Francine, Renee, and Terri for lending your eyes and thoughts to this material and to our teachers, mentors and guides. Deborah sends her love to her Mom and Dad for their absolute belief in all she does and to her family, both two legged and four legged with a special hug to her shining knight! Miranda sends her love to everyone that reads this book and applies the exercises to their life. Also to my both spiritual and relative family for their support and belief in me, and especially my mother and my son because without them my contribution of this book would not be possible.

Table of Contents

The Diet and Weight Loss Industry

Today, the Diet Industry is one of the fastest growing industries in America. It seems that all one has to do is put the words "Diet" or "Weight Loss" on the cover of a new book and they've got a hit on their hands. Interestingly the Diet Industry also has the highest failure rate of any industry in the world, with a 95 – 98% percent failure rate! Statistics show that most people who lose weight through the use of a pill, shake, diet or "system" gain all of that weight back, and even a few extra pounds, within three years. Imagine what would happen to the automotive industry if it had such a failure rate. Or a doctor? Imagine you had a 95% failure rate at your own job? You (and they) would be out of business! So why does the Diet Industry continue to thrive and grow despite its record of failure? In the case of pills or shakes, the turn around time between the loss of fifteen pounds and the gain of twenty can be just a few months. This reality is both devastating to a person's self esteem as well as physical health.

The biggest explanation for this sad and sorry situation is the simple truth that the Diet and Weight Loss Industry primarily markets itself on the premise of false hope. It would seem that people are willing to believe that all they have to do is participate in this magic formula and they will somehow have the body they've always wanted.   If one formula doesn't work, have no fear, there are many more to choose from. Just drink this, take that, count those, and on and on it goes like a volatile roller coaster that never seems to end.

The Role You Play in All of This?

Since the Diet and Weight Loss Industry is based on false hope resulting in failure almost all the time, it is necessary to redirect the challenge of successful weight loss back to the individual.   You may feel you are caught in a helpless situation, but you are far from helpless! In fact, you are a powerful being who is capable of great things. When you believe this, you will no longer be seduced by the idea of "something for nothing." Instead, you will value yourself highly enough on the self-care scale to begin the process of consciously caring for your body, which will lead you to finally achieve the body you want and keep it!

What's that Weight About Anyway?

Have you ever really thought about why you carry more weight than you are comfortable with? Of course, the typical culprits -- overeating, eating junk foods or fast foods, and lack of physical activity -- are definitely part and parcel of being overweight; each of those readily-apparent causes is usually the end result of something else going on under the surface.

Sometimes particular medical conditions can play a role in weight gain, which need to be acknowledged and understood. For others of us, the hidden causes are instead psychological, such as habits formed in childhood around eating. How many of us can recall being told to finish what's on our plates because of the hungry children in the world? Perhaps our parents themselves had weight issues, or we were soothed when crying with food. Maybe were taught to band aide pain by having something sweet. One of the most common themes we have come across consistently in explaining extra weight is the hiding of problems and pain by burying it somewhere deep inside, otherwise known as emotional hiding. Events happen in all of our lives that can lead us to believe that we are not enough, that we are wrong, bad or somehow inadequate (low self-esteem or self-value). Often these events happen in early childhood, and the negative ideas they "teach" us become ways in which we pattern our lives to try and compensate for our imagined shortcomings and wrong doings.

Statistics also show us the sad but real fact that many of us experience some form of abuse be it emotional, physical or sexual, and that this abuse also imprints on our subconscious as we attempt to "deal" with these issues. Often we just disconnect in whole or in part and end up being a member of the walking wounded, doing everything we can to fill the unquenchable void this creates. Some deal with this by attempting to fill themselves with relationship after relationship. Some become workaholics and/or alcoholics. More than a few form dysfunctional eating habits, turning to "comfort" food as a way of feeling better, only it never lasts and never really gets better. This type of disconnection is the culprit for each failed attempt to obtain the body you think you want because you can never out-perform your self-image. So even if you do find a formula that assists you in losing weight, it isn't permanent because the fix isn't happening at an emotional level. It's not addressing the real reason for the weight, and that's like putting a band aide on an untreated infection. It doesn't heal anything.

While losing weight and fitting into that particular size you've been dreaming of may feel great, what many have discovered once they achieve this is that it doesn't cut it long-term. They still have trouble feeling better on a consistent basis, nor does it make them feel valuable or worthy. Really, all they've become is a smaller size. Often when someone succeeds in losing weight, they end up feeling better about who they are, and while on the surface this is certainly a good thing, one can never outperform their self-image. In other words, if you believe you are flawed, or bad, or simply not good enough, old habits will ultimately win over any other changes you've managed to make in order to properly align you with how you view yourself. Thus, any boost to their self- esteem ends up being just like will power. Eventually it burns out and old habits resurface.

It's almost as if somewhere inside a voice starts to say that they don't deserve to feel good, they don't deserve to look good, they don't deserve to feel better. While they may manage to wrestle with this for a while, the voice is tireless. It eventually overpowers the situation and boom the weight starts crawling back up.

Of course, issues with weight can also go in other directions when it comes to realizing low self-esteem. One may not fall back into old patterns, but instead, redirect them into more controlling and self destructive behaviors by binging and purging, or starving themselves.   Just like carrying too much weight can be very harmful to the body, eating disorders are incredibly disabling and dangerous.   In either case, the solution cries out for addressing the underlying causes of the problem.

The Good News...

It doesn't have to be like this!

The information contained in this workbook has been created with a few intentions. First, to discover any unhealthy eating habits, thought patterns and/or beliefs that no longer serve you. Second, we have opened the door of self exploration to assist in uncovering any causes or reasons you may be hiding, which will remove inner barriers and allow for healing to begin. This will allow you to step off the roller coaster and regain perspective, establishing a new beginning of self acceptance, forgiveness and love and actually supporting you through the process of emotional discovery and release.

The principles taught here are simple. When you feel better about who you are right now, this minute, you will make better choices. You will naturally start to do things that will serve you. You will begin to take better care and ultimately you will succeed in allowing that healthy, vibrant and beautiful body you absolutely deserve. The best part is: These changes will be permanent.

The concepts shared in this workbook are based wholly on the writers' two very different but poignant journeys regarding weight, self-esteem, emotional healing, and the manifestation of self-love — in other words, our two different journeys to allowing for a healthy body. While our journeys may have been different, the reality for both authors is that it wasn't until we realized our own personal power and worth that we were able to achieve and sustain a physical body we feel good living in. Through our many years of healing work, life coaching and spiritual practice, we have also assisted many others in achieving the same.

It is our greatest wish that this workbook will open the door to all the possibilities in your life by allowing you to gain deeper insight into who you think you are. When you begin to expose your beliefs, you become capable of changing them. You become able to change your perception, which allows you to release and ultimately heal. This journey takes you to a place where you are no longer a victim to something you don't understand but rather, you become a wonderful and amazing being who absolutely achieves and deserves the body that serves you in perfect health. (By the way, this also includes awakening to a life and lifestyle that inspires you and likewise everyone around you.)

This is a process. It will not happen overnight and it will happen. The only element that must be in place for you to enter your doorway to true and lasting success is commitment. The best part is: It isn't a commitment to a diet, or a philosophy that someone else is telling you will work. No, what we are talking about is a commitment to your self to self-discovery, healing and self-creation. This is about you being in the driver's seat and choosing your destination. We will help you design your road map; just be persistent and consistent, and allow yourself whatever traveling time it takes to arrive at your destination.

You will get there.   Are you ready?

Note: It is important to understand that what you eat does matter. It matters that you learn to make healthier choices, eat more organic and whole or live foods, start to say "no" to fast foods and junk foods, cut back on desserts, stop all artificial sweeteners, and discover Stevia or Agave, Nectar, and so on. Slowly eliminate sodas, replacing them with healthy juices, (please read labels and note that contains 10% real juice doesn't qualify as a healthy juice. Look for 100% juice blends) herbal teas and water. These and other such behaviors should not be negated but rather embraced as an important part of this healing process and transformation. Likewise, going for walks, climbing stairs versus using the elevator, and starting an exercise class are also all part and parcel of gaining good health.   Don't worry as you begin to move through the process shared in this workbook, you will find yourself actually wanting to do these things and more.

One further word is important to share. As we mentioned earlier, there are some medical conditions and medications or treatments that can result in weight gain. It is important to see your Doctor to make sure that the intentions you set for yourself are not hindered by something medical that can be addressed if you know about it. Also, when starting a workout or a health regime, it can be very important to check in with your Doctor and/or a personal trainer who is properly educated and can guide you when you first start out. Be sure to take care of your whole person and you will experience whole results.

The Power of Our Thoughts

For us to understand the power of our thoughts we must first take a deeper look at what that really means. Have you ever wondered what a thought really is? A thought is the first step in the manifestation process. Without thought we would not possess the ability to communicate, as we know it, because it's the thought that creates the words. While it is possible to speak without thinking, typically we think first about what we are about to say. Thoughts get generated from many different stimuli, and they can come up at anytime. Sometimes it's something someone has said or something we've read, and sometimes it just seems to come from within us like a point of inspiration. Some call this divine guidance; others call this type of inspired thought a connection to the higher self. Whatever you may believe, when the thought originates from within, it a creation that comes from you. The more conscious a person becomes, the more her or his thoughts can be self-originated. Ultimately these are the thoughts we want to listen to and take action on because these are the ones that are in alignment with our highest good.   When we feel badly about ourselves, we can rest assured that to some degree we are thinking thoughts that are dis-empowering and non-supportive.

Why would we want to think negative and unsupportive thoughts? Right now, many of the thoughts you are thinking are coming through your own personal filtering system, and that filtering system is your perception. Your perception is based upon your prior life experiences. When you think about it, two people can watch the same movie and have totally different perceptions regarding the movie's message or a particular character; those differing perceptions are based on their different life experiences and their personal filtering system. The same can be said for conversations that turn into disagreements or arguments. Both people participating in the argument have brought their own personal filtering system to the table and therefore are only hearing what the other is saying based on what is getting through their own personal filter. Distorted hearing is all too often the result. Do you remember having a conversation with someone and it seems as if they only hearing what they want to hear? This is what we are talking about! What you are saying to that person is being processed through his or her filtering system. In short, our personal filtering system places our hearing on autopilot when whatever we are receiving is being processed in this way.

It is almost impossible not to be reactive and argumentative until we realize that what we are reacting to isn't the moment – rather, we are reacting to the past, and the past is not relevant to this moment. This disengages our personal filtering system and allows us to participate in what is actually happening right now. In essence we reclaim our power and our thoughts whenever we disengage our personal filtering system and allow ourselves to be in present time.

When our personal filtering system becomes so overwhelming that it literally alters our perceptions to the point of disabling our thoughts, some people find themselves walking down the dark road of depression. Science has shown us that our brain literally wires itself together based on thoughts and feelings that we have the majority of the time. If we have lots of happy thoughts and good feelings, our brain tends to wire itself in that direction. If we are in pain, angry and/or unhappy, the brain will wire itself in that direction and we will be prone to more of the same. There are many mysteries within the bio-chemical universe that we will not explore at this time; if you want to learn more about these things, we encourage you to do so. The great news is this: Wherever you may be in this moment through using your thoughts, your brain will literally rewire itself to be in alignment with you! This is the incredible power you possess.

Our thoughts can be our greatest supporters or our greatest disablers. Anything you see around you, simple or complex, was first a thought before it was anything else. This is how powerful thoughts can be. To truly understand how your thoughts are working with you at this time, it is very important to begin the process of exposing them. It is absolutely important to do this in loving and gentle ways, which this workbook will assist you in doing, and it's important that this work be seen as a key part of who you are and who you choose to be.

Your personal filtering system is a key ingredient in your personal belief systems, and as you gain more and more understanding of what these things are, you can begin to release your personal filtering system (or expand it to include limitless possibilities). You can begin to reshape your belief systems and think thoughts that are in alignment with what you want.

Often we address our needs with the firepower of our will, otherwise known as will power, and sometimes this strategy can take us pretty far. But it will never get us all the way (and help us stay there) because our will power will burn out. What this means is that you can apply your will towards achieving what you want or reaching a goal you have set, and for some this will get you to the gate. Others may get half way there before their will power short circuits. Still others find that their will power burns out before they ever get started! And even those who have exercised their will a great deal day-to-day may actually achieve what they want -- they may indeed obtain their goal -- but that's as far as it goes. They expended so much will power in getting there that it is simply not strong enough to allow them to maintain. Think of your will power as a rechargeable battery: at some point it will need to be recharged. This is where you will be stopped every time if you rely solely upon your will to get things done. Ultimately, will power can be considered a tool to assist us on our journey, but it is not the fuel to get us there.

Bottom line: Our thoughts are so powerful that they not only affect our internal universe, they actually affect our external universe as well. An interesting example of how thoughts can create our experiences in the world is as follows: a customer service representative was at work answering the phone and assisting customers in all aspects of ordering groceries online and having the groceries delivered to the customer's home. When a customer called trying to find a specific item on the grocer's website which repeated searches could not find, the customer insisted she was certain it was on the website, and furthermore, she always ordered it. The customer was irritated and repeatedly complained about how she absolutely did not have time for this. The interesting thing was that each time the rep and the customer each typed the product into the website's search engine, the sales rep brought the item up every time, in fact it was the first item displayed, but the customer who was complaining about how she didn't have time didn't get the same result.

This is a prime example of how the customer's thoughts created her direct external experience, and the more resistance she exhibited, the harder and longer the process became. In short, she kept affirming that she didn't have time for this, so the universe kept obliging her, creating an experience that made real her impatient statement and gave her less and less time for finding the item she wanted.

The question to ask right now is: "How am I doing this in my life?" Meaning, how are you affirming things you don't want to have happen in your world today? Consider this carefully, journal about it, and realize that everything you focus on, be it good, bad or indifferent, you will receive in some level. So, what do you want to focus on? If the customer could have taken a deep breath and come to a place of peace (maybe stopped what she was doing for a few minutes and regroup), in essence letting go of her belief about her lack of time, odds are she would have quickly and effortlessly found what she was looking for.

Another great example of the power of thought that also feeds into the law of attraction is highlighted in a great movie entitled "What the Bleep Do We Know," a documentary about Quantum Physics and learning how to love ourselves. In the movie there is a scene that describes the work of Dr. Emoto entitled "The Hidden Messages in Water." In his work he tested water from different sources including distilled, or what some would consider lifeless water. He contained the water and then put a word or sentence on the container. He later measured the results those words or sentences had on the waters structure by taking pictures of the water crystals. The tests revealed that when a positive word, or sentence was placed upon the water, even the distilled water, the crystal formations became quite beautiful. (In the case of the distilled water, it was as if the words or sentences brought the so-called "lifeless" water back to life.) The word "Love" incited an incredible image in the water crystals that truly defies description. When a negative word or sentence like "Hate" or "I Want to Kill You" was used, the crystals in the water became distorted and ugly. This is really powerful when you consider the fact we are made up of somewhere between 70 and 90 percent water, depending on who you study. It makes us realize that our thoughts can be creating beauty and harmony within our very cells, or distortion and ugliness.

How does the power of our thoughts affect our body? There may not be a more powerful representation about how our thoughts can literally damage our cells than the water studies of Dr. Emoto so it may be something you want to look up and inwardly digest further and on a deeper level. We will attempt to put what we know to be true in this regard into a simple statement: If you think good thoughts, you will have good feelings. If you think loving thoughts, you will have loving feelings. If you attempt to adjust your thinking just a fraction of a millimeter in the direction of good and loving thoughts, you will notice in a very short time that you will be feeling better and acting more loving towards yourself and others.

Simple enough? No one says that is going to be easy, but it is a very simple process when you understand that how you think about yourself basically dictates your feelings and experiences. Yes, you are that powerful. There may be things you don't even know you are thinking. There may be personal filtering systems and belief systems you don't know you have. But as the process in this workbook illustrates, these things will begin to reveal themselves the minute you start doing this work. It will take a little time to completely expose your personal filtering system, and this filtering system may indeed extend into every area of your life, but with love, forgiveness and acceptance, step by step and day by day you will wake up to discover that it is indeed possible to have the body you want and the life you want.

What Are You Thinking?

When you really think about it, our thoughts have a huge impact on our emotions. In order to become someone who is practicing self-love, self-respect and self-care, we must also realize that a large part of this successful transformation comes back to our thoughts. Tending to our thoughts and emotions can clue us in to the choices we've been making around our health and our habits. Once we recognize the habits and patterns that do not serve us, we can begin to make better choices that will serve us -- such as eating good food.

We've probably all heard the saying, "We are our own worst enemy," and it's true! We can be our harshest critic and worst supporter without even realizing it.   Now comes the turnaround as we learn to forgive, release, allow and love ourselves anyway. This amazing change will start a new relationship for us and even allow us to become our greatest friend, most loving supporter and ally.

Another familiar saying is: "Do unto others what you would have them do onto you." Based on what we've just shared with you, and guessing that you actually treat others better than yourself, we suggest that you begin to treat yourself the way you treat others! It will work in all directions when you begin to treat yourself with loving-kindness; others will begin to do so as well.

A Comedic Approach!

Let's stop for a minute and take a look at the Three Stooges. Yes, we say with a laugh, the Three Stooges -- the timeless comedy trio that is the infamous Larry, Curly and Moe. If you don't know them, you will find their movies in the classics section of your movie rental store. (And while we're at it, let's also suggest that laughter is also a key component to releasing weight and being healthy in mind, body and spirit.)

Now, let's play a game and pretend that you are in charge of caring for one of the three characters that work seamlessly together in all of their routines. Larry wouldn't be Larry — or even that funny -- if Curly and Moe weren't there too. If any piece of this comedic trio were missing from the whole, it wouldn't work at all. So if you're taking care of Larry, you would have to take care of all three of them equally because none of them work without the other two. If you don't take care of the whole, neither the whole nor any of its parts work any longer. They were known as the Three Stooges for a reason!

Why did we go off on this seeming tangent about a comedy trio that is famous for their collective slapstick? Because it's a great representation of how you are functioning, and how your thoughts either work together and support each other, or they don't. If you only pay attention to one part of the picture, the results will end up being incomplete, just like a punch line losing all humor because there was only one stooge to deliver it. The most important part of all of this is to realize that taking care of the whole being, all thoughts, self-talk, resistance and personal belief systems is the Magic when it comes to redirecting and recreating who you are. This is all part of becoming who you choose to be, of becoming healthy, happy and all that good stuff you think you would really like to have working in your life. (Remember to laugh, smile and in general keep your sense of humor along the way. Go rent a fun comedy and just laugh; in fact laugh out loud and often!)

So let's explore our concepts around self talk and personal belief systems, we will touch on resistance a little further on.

Self Talk

Self-talk can look – or sound – like this: "You are so stupid!" "Who do you think you are?" "You'll never get it right," or "Who are you kidding? You are not good enough and you never will be." We could go on, and you could surely add your own self-talk examples here as well, but you probably get the point. Realistically, when any of us get caught up in this type of self-sabotaging conversation, we usually do go on and on. This is something we truly must recognize and change over time.

This is where the art of becoming the observer in our own life is so important, because as you practice self-observation you start to become aware of what you're saying, and once you are able to hear these self defacing, sometimes painful and negative statements, you can begin to tune into how they make you feel. Begin to pay attention deep down at your gut level and ask yourself, "How am I feeling?" "Do I really want to feel like that?" If the answer is "no", you can begin to make another choice that will allow you to feel better. The more you practice this, the easier it will become. Give yourself time to learn this new habit of observation and put it into practice, and one day in the not too distant future, you will find yourself actually saying encouraging and supportive things to yourself without even thinking about it.

Write down some of the things that you say to yourself that don't make you feel good.

_____

_____

_____

_____

_____

Based on what you just wrote above, write down things that would be your new choice for how you are going to talk to yourself and allow yourself to feel good.

_____

_____

_____

_____

_____

Use this simple exercise in clarity any time to help you in reinforcing positive self-talk.

Before we move on we have to address an important reality, which is how your self-talk about other people really impacts you. Often we make the mistake of thinking that when we think or talk about others it isn't affecting us. What we are not seeing is that <u>we</u> are the ones receiving whatever energy we put out, regardless of how it may be directed. How about when you're talking about someone at the office, a neighbor, or even a stranger in a store? For example: "What a jerk!" or, "I don't like... (fill in the name)," or "She/he is so stuck up!" Then there's the everyday experience of getting cut off on the road: "You crazy driver; who do you think you are?" When we are putting out negative or angry thoughts of self talk like this, directed at someone else, what we are actually doing is creating negative energy in our own bodies and as a result, becoming a magnet attracting more of it into our lives. In essence, we are picking up and carrying more baggage every time we generate more negativity... not the task we want to be doing when our goal is to release.

To create a better body, better health, a better lifestyle and in the end, a better world, we must first start with ourselves. Gandhi said it best when he said: "We must become the change we seek." What we are saying here is: When we generate negative energy in our bodies, we end up falling into bad habits and unhealthful activities. When we do things that make us feel bad, we end up saying to ourselves things like, "Who cares what I eat?", or "It doesn't matter doing something good for myself, right?

Write down some of the things you have said or thought about other people that may not be leading you down a positive path.

_____

_____

_____

_____

_____

Based on what you have written above, take some of things you have said about others and shift them to a positive statement. Remember, what you put out is what you get back.

_____

_____

_____

_____

_____

Belief Systems

Let's take a minute now to look at belief systems. While the phrase or idea of a belief system may not be foreign to you, for the most part people have difficulty when it comes to explaining what a belief system is. A belief system is a series of thoughts about ourselves, and what we think it takes to get what we want or desire in life.

The truth is, we all deserve to have a happy, fulfilling, loving, incredible, and prosperous life. Meantime, while we may deserve these things, many of us wake up each day and find that this isn't the life we are living. The reasons for this can be many fold and the one common and key ingredient is, without question, a belief system at work running your life. The hardest part of all is that most of us have bought into our belief systems unknowingly or perhaps better said, unconsciously. Our belief systems start out innocently enough as a reaction to something that has happened; however, over time, they become imbedded into our consciousness and we start to believe that our belief system is simply the way life is. This is a dangerous stand to take because it typically feeds limitation, lack and doubt.

Before we go any further, let's understand better how this happened. Usually our belief systems are all wrapped around occurrences, experiences and events that happened, beginning in our childhood and continuing on through our lives. Often the most pivotal belief we hold happened to us at a time when we didn't even know what was going on; we only knew that something didn't feel right. A belief system may have been born when you were crying as a little child and no one came to comfort you. From that experience you may have decided you weren't valuable enough for anyone to take the time to care for you, and now you are an adult who thinks she or he doesn't need anyone. Another example could be when you came home from school with a "B" on your report card, and your Mom or Dad said, "Why didn't you get an A?" From that moment on, you decided you weren't good enough, and now you are a classic over-achiever with low self esteem.

It's important to understand that these beliefs came from a moment when you thought something was wrong. As children we don't conceive of the idea that something could happen around us that has nothing to do with us. We see ourselves as the source of all things, which is both a gift and a curse because we can't separate ourselves from something that has nothing to do with us. When something happens and we experience a change in our safe wonderful reality that is supposed to be childhood, our immediate survival instinct is to do whatever we can, whatever it takes, to restore our safe, wonderful reality. We take it on as if it's ours to fix, and then we change something about who we are and how we behave in order to accomplish our task. Thus, a belief system is born. And as we grow, our belief system grows too, because everything we experience from that point forward is reinforced by that initial decision, and life will always show up to meet our unconscious expectations. You may have become the care giver, the rebel, the quiet one that tries hard not to be any trouble, and so on. This is where belief systems come from and they will run our lives for as long as we let them.

Most of our initial belief systems, which the rest of our belief systems are later based upon, came out of our basic survival instincts. If we want to do more than survive, we must begin to recognize our belief systems, take them on (decide whether or not they are real) and reinvent them.

Let's also understand that while we can review our childhood and point fingers at how mom, dad, grandma or sis did this or that to us, for the most part, everyone in our lives was doing the best they could, just as we were. People unknowingly and unconsciously pass along legacies — habits and patterns — because they aren't awake enough to realize what they are doing. We can't do much about that; we can only wake ourselves up and in the case of our children, decide that the legacy stops with us.

So let's look at reinventing belief systems. First, it is not until we start living our life in awareness and observing what we do, that we can start to uncover what belief systems we have taken on. Congratulations for being in this place right now!

Examples of what you may uncover can be as follows: "I must work 60 hours a week to make this much money" or, "No matter how hard I work there's never enough." How about "I have to please everyone and make them happy for them to like me", or one of our favorites: "I have to be good for them to love me". Does any of this sound childish to you? This is because we first "learn" these ideas in childhood, which means many of us are making extremely important decisions about our lives and our futures based on the belief systems we created at four and five years old! As children, we pretty much had to do as we were told, but here is the good news -- we are not children any more. We are all grown up, and now we get to decide what works for us today based on what we choose for ourselves today. This is how you change or transform belief systems: you give yourself permission – now that you are all grown up – to create a new belief system that actually serves your life.

Until we allow ourselves to do this, our belief systems can suffocate us and feed bad habits that lead us down dark alleys on cold and lonely nights. (Excuse the added drama, but it helps to make the point.) Belief systems can all run us into the ground mentally, emotionally and physically.

In order to understand how releasing your own belief systems can make a change in you, let's start by taking a look at the people closest to you. Let's say there is someone in that group who is a people pleaser. This person is usually the one offering to do everything and asking for no help whatsoever. When you have determined who that person is, ask yourself this question: if she or he didn't come from a place of having to please people all the time, would you still want to know them? Most the time the answer is YES. Well then, if you are willing to let them be someone different and you know you would still like them or even love them, then it's good reinforcement that others around you will allow for the same transformation in you. More importantly, if you can offer that level of acceptance for someone else, you can offer it to yourself. It all just takes a little practice.

What is your belief system around your weight? Your health? Your over all body image? Take a moment and write down your immediate thoughts.

_____

_____

_____

_____

_____

_____

Congratulate yourself for your courage. ☺

Let's look even closer now at how you recognize that you have a belief system, and how you get rid of the beliefs that don't serve you once you have identified them. Start by tuning into your heart when it comes to something you think you want to do. What are your reasons for wanting to do it? Are you attached to the outcome, or the means by which you will get it? Really tune into how this feels -- the more you do this, the more you will feel and learn about who you are and how you have functioned up until now.

If you don't already keep a journal, now is a great time to start. You will learn more about yourself on this journey of self discovery, and faster, if you start writing about what you are experiencing and ultimately what you want to experience. If you don't have a journal yet, just go get one; any inexpensive notebook will do. You'll learn to love it. You'll even get to go back later and see how much you've grown. If you find there are things you don't want to keep, rip those pages out and burn them, or throw them away. It's your journal and you can do with it what you want!

When you start by tuning into your heart and your reaction to things that are happening around you, notice if your reaction feels good to you. If you feel you are in a good place, then whatever belief system may be supporting that place is serving you. If, however, you feel bad, anxious or upset, chances are there is a belief system at work that is not of service to you or your well being.

To illustrate, here are a couple of examples you may find helpful. First, a woman named Mary goes out to buy a new outfit. She tries on quite a few as she tends to be fairly critical about how clothes look on her. Finally she finds one she thinks will work. When she gets home she puts it on to show her husband, hoping he will like it. As she puts it on and before she shows her hubby, she starts to think that maybe her body doesn't look as good as she thought it did in this outfit; maybe it isn't such a great outfit after all. While this is going on, her husband, who is always telling her how beautiful she is, encourages her to show him how great she looks. Mary steps into the living room and does a slow turn showing him the outfit. "What do you think?", she asks, although the critic within her is already answering the question, telling her she doesn't look good at all. He looks at the outfit and his beautiful wife and replies, "It looks great." Suddenly Mary finds herself being irritated by his simple response and accuses him of just saying that to spare her feelings because it doesn't look good at all. She runs out of the room believing her internal critic, which is born from a belief system that has convinced her she looks terrible.

This is a perfect example of an unconscious belief system that does not serve Mary and feels bad. If Mary were to explore this reaction a little deeper she would probably find the reason for feeling so badly about herself. This would allow her to heal that wounded part of herself, which in turn would silence her inner critic and allow her to feel better about herself. Does any of this sound familiar? (No worries if it does, it's called being human!)

In another example, a woman named Cheryl decides she wants to bake a cake for an upcoming birthday gathering. She won't bake just any cake, but one she considers herself famous for, a cake that always gets rave reviews whenever she serves it. In fact, Cheryl feels so obligated to contribute to this occasion that she offers to make the birthday cake and insists that the hostess cancel any other plans for any other birthday cake. Cheryl has a lot of friends she is always doing things for, and this is no exception. The hostess, of course, happily agrees, as it is one less thing for her to do. Cheryl goes shopping for her ingredients and makes plans to prepare the cake over the next two evenings, as it is a very detailed process.

The next morning Cheryl has a crisis at work that takes all of her time and attention until late that evening and then carries into the next day. She has to work late two days in a row, which means her baking schedule is completely thrown off. Needless to say, Cheryl becomes totally stressed out about the cake she has committed to, which is now not prepared or prepped in any way.

Feeling completely pressured, Cheryl stays up all night after two stress-filled days at work and attempts to make her cake. The only problem is that instead of loving the process as she usually does, Cheryl is tired and becomes resentful that she should be expected to bake this birthday cake when everyone knows how busy she is. By the end of the night, the cake is made and Cheryl is convinced the hostess should never have agreed to let her do such a thing. She gets about an hour's sleep and goes to work feeling totally taken advantage of. By the time the party rolls around, Cheryl is so tired and angry about the whole situation that she actually drops off the cake and doesn't even attend the party she had so wanted to enjoy.

The first thing we want to examine is: What was driving Cheryl to insist she make the birthday cake and then put herself through so much to get it done when at any point there were other options? Perhaps there was a belief system at work here telling Cheryl she has to take care of her friends or they won't like her. And if this were her belief system, it would follow that not only could she not take the easier route and order a cake, as this would be seen in her eyes as a failure, but she would also end up resenting the entire situation because in the clutches of a belief system like this one, if she doesn't deliver, she isn't appreciated or liked.

Can you relate to this scenario, or do you know someone like this? It's also safe to imagine that if Cheryl were to examine her reactions, she would soon realize that this way of being was making her feel bad and was not serving her. When we get to a point where we understand when things are not serving us, we become able to move beyond the bad feelings and cultivate better ones, and over time, we can cultivate more supportive and loving belief systems. If you allow yourself to begin to let go of your negative belief systems, you start living a life filled with love, inspiration, and joy.

In short, a belief system is based on what you believe to be the truth about yourself and your experiences. Pay attention to how you are feeling and you will start to discern what is working for you and what isn't. When you establish this type of inner connection, you are empowered to create new and good choices for yourself that ultimately have you feeling great.

Now take another moment and review what you wrote above about your belief systems. Review them and ask yourself: how could I change those beliefs to be five percent more supportive, just five percent? Write down what comes to mind and continue to work with this idea daily — increments can be as small or as large as you want — until you reach one hundred percent supportive beliefs.

_____

_____

_____

_____

_____

_____

_____

_____

_____

(Work through these daily, or as often as you can, in your journal!)

Attracting the Body You Want

Below are a series of concepts, exercises and philosophies. Please take the time to review and participate fully in each area, as these simple steps will place you on the road to ultimate success.

Whole: *Dictionary Definition (adj): Complete, including all parts or aspects, with nothing left out. Not wounded, impaired, or incapacitated. Healed or restored to health physically or psychologically.*

What does the word "whole" mean to you?

_____

_____

_____

Our definition is best explained by taking action. To be whole, you must take the action to recognize those places within you that are like an energy vortex, or emotional void. These places demand to be filled in order to validate some form of your existence, and their appetite for validation is unceasing. When these places within are exposed, loved, forgiven, and accepted, and when you take your power away from their dysfunction by choosing to be functional, you are becoming whole. To be whole is to be healed. Please write the following statement:, "I deserve to be whole."

_____

Love: *Dictionary Definition (n): An intense feeling of tender affection and compassion. Something that elicits deep interest and enthusiasm in somebody. The mercy, grace and charity shown as in God to humanity. The Score in a tennis match!*

What does the word "love" mean to you?

_____

_____

_____

Our definition is once again best described in an action that would be, first and foremost, learning the art of loving yourself. Love is a wonderful feeling and experience to share, but in order to experience or share love to its fullest capacity, one must truly understand the power in first loving oneself.

When you read these words, take a moment and tune into how they feel. Self-love is often criticized and deemed selfish. This is untrue. Self-love is the only way we can ever succeed at being a loving person and truly giving love to others and to the world. Love comes from within when we understand and give ourselves permission to forgive the past. Love comes from compassion and patience and letting go. Love is found in letting go of all the "could haves, would haves, and should haves," all the "not good enoughs, didn't do it rights, not worthys" and all the other bull that clutters up our hearts and disconnects us from the truth of our magnificence. Love is freedom, and grace. It's the ability to allow everyone, especially ourselves, to be who they are, who we are, right now and love them -- love ourselves -- anyway! Love is the purest power that will allow you to achieve anything.

Please write: "With love I can achieve anything."

_____

Respect: *Dictionary Definition (n): A feeling or attitude of admiration and deference towards somebody or something. Consideration or thoughtfulness.*

What does the word "respect" mean to you?

_____

_____

_____

_____

_____

As in our definition of love, we again add the word "self" to the equation, and define respect first with the act of self-respect. In order to truly achieve anything, we must first believe we can. If we have little or no respect for ourselves, it stands to reason we are not going to fully believe in our abilities and therefore not be able to fully achieve. This can result in a lot of one step forward, two steps back scenarios which can become so self defeating we eventually give up; this in turn feeds our beliefs that we aren't good enough or deserving. Respecting yourself means allowing yourself the opportunity to grow, to make mistakes and continue to move forward. Self-respect includes having self-supporting thoughts and words to ourselves, versus that non-supportive chatter that you would never in a million years say to somebody else but for some reason seem routinely OK with saying to yourself. While you might have come to believe something about yourself based on your past experiences, this does not mean that the past has any power over you today. Learning to respect yourself means putting your feelings first. It means that you have enough value to ask for what you require, and that you will take care of yourself by recognizing and releasing toxic behaviors. Self-respect means that you will aspire to feel good on a regular basis. When you practice self respect, you will begin to feel better, better and better.

Please write: "As I respect myself, I feel good. As I practice self-respect, I feel better, better and better."

_____

_____

_____

Release: *Dictionary Definition (vt): To set free. To stop gripping or holding something. To let out something that has been contained or confined within something or pent up or latent inside somebody. To take tension off...*

What does the word "release" mean to you?

_____

_____

_____

_____

Our definition of release is simply to let go. Letting go is not easy, but it is a simple act that when carried out creates room for the new. New experiences, new emotions, new outcomes and whole new possibilities are all possible once the past has been released or let go of. Holding onto something more accurately becomes holding in something, and when we emotionally warehouse our experiences and emotions, rather than express them and let them go, we literally can carry around all the weight of those unspoken emotions, unexpressed sadness, anger and rage, unrequited feelings and self defeating beliefs, bad experiences, angry self sabotaging chatter and deep emotional wounds. Losing weight may appear to be easy on the surface, but when the weight comes from all of these emotionally suppressed thoughts and feelings, it's not hard to see how deep and difficult it actually is to let that weight go. After all, this is weight that has built up around you to house all this emotional baggage and perhaps to protect you — a person who was sexually abused, for example, may hide inside of their weight in order not to be seen, so as not to be viewed sexually by the next potential abuser. So you see, the weight loss we speak of is not about the next greatest diet, but rather about healing from within and releasing on an emotional level first. It's about finding and forgiving, healing the wounds, exposing the dysfunctions and realizing that right now, today, you are safe. There is a lot involved in the process of releasing; however we know it to be key in manifesting the body you want and the life you desire.

Please write: "I allow myself to release a little more each day, knowing I am safe."

_____

_____

Forgiveness: *Dictionary Definition (n): The act of pardoning somebody for a mistake or wrongdoing. The tendency to forgive offences readily and easily. From the root "Forgive"; to stop being angry or resentful.*

What does the word "forgiveness" mean to you?

_____

_____

_____

_____

_____

Forgiveness as seen by us is the magical act that allows a bold new future to become possible. Forgiveness is not an act done in the name of another person, or even for their benefit; it is done for our own well-being, and for ourselves. If we do not forgive, we carry the anger, grief, disappointment and hurt. Allow me to repeat that: If we do not forgive we carry the anger, grief, disappointment and hurt -- and you can probably guess where we carry it! It's important to understand that forgiving someone or something does not make what they did okay, nor does it mean you have to put yourself into anything that would allow another who has hurt you the opportunity to do it again. Forgiveness is a coming to terms with the past and the present. It is the only way to release it, and it is letting yourself off the hook by allowing you to move beyond whatever event or action you have forgiven.

Forgiveness comes from love and with compassion. It allows for peace rather then pain. No one has to ask for your forgiveness in order for you to give it; it is only your decision. Often those we are angry with don't even know why we are angry because they have gone beyond whatever event we are stuck on.   Forgiveness also means we can let go of anger because in the case of anger it will not remain unexpressed indefinitely. In holding on to anger, we will eventually end up blowing up at some convenient, probably unrelated person or event while continuing to beat up on ourselves because anger is simply inclined in this direction. What better way to continue to beat yourself up and then gain another five pounds? Yes, forgiveness is a courageous act, but it is also the most precious gift you can give to yourself. Forgive and let go.

Please write: "I give myself permission to give myself the precious gift of forgiveness. I forgive and let go."

_____

_____

_____

Peace: *Dictionary Definition (n): A time when a war or conflict ends. Freedom from conflict.. A state of mental calm and serenity, no anxiety. The absence of violence or other disturbances...*

What does the word "peace" mean to you?

_____

_____

_____

_____

_____

Peace within means that self-love, self-acceptance, forgiveness, self-care and support are our natural state of being. In a state of peace, our bodies also become at peace within themselves and gravitate to their natural state of greatest health, with our participation. To be at peace means we respect our bodies and ourselves, and when we have self-respect, we treat ourselves in healthful, loving ways. To have peace within is to be whole. It means coming to terms with, and releasing the past, and moving towards the future you choose free of any and all burdens.

When you are truly at peace with where you are right now, you cease fighting yourself, and when you cease that battle you have won. It's only a matter of time before you reap the rewards. To be in battle with the self is only damaging and destructive because whom you are fighting with is yourself -- your body -- and this creates a very negative and degenerative environment that can encourage breakdown and even sickness. To be at peace is to be in a place of allowing, it lets all good in, it allows for deep healing and encourages the body on a cellular level to move towards all things that feel good. When you feel good, you are on the right track. You will naturally begin to do the things that allow you to feel better, and the better you feel, the better you will take care of yourself. It all becomes its own habit or pattern. Let us give up battling our weight and let's be at peace. When we are peaceful, we are powerful and now everything is possible.

(To us, peace is the ultimate answer, the real truth of our health and well being. Of course we are speaking of internal peace which reflects externally once it is achieved. One who has found peace, will always choose peace, making a world in peace more a reality with every peaceful decision. When just enough find peace within, peace on earth is possible.)

Please write: "I'm at peace, I'm powerful, I'm safe and everything is possible."

_____

Gratitude: *Dictionary Definition (n): a feeling of being thankful.*

What does the word "gratitude" mean to you?

_____

_____

_____

_____

If there is any secret out there waiting to be discovered that will unlock every door and move through any resistance, it is the art of gratitude. Being thankful is essential to attracting anything you desire. Being thankful is your ticket to a prosperous and healthy life, great body, great relationships and even great income! When you surround yourself with gratitude for all that you have and all you are attracting, you begin to change the way your energy is vibrating.

Energy is always vibrating; it is the essence of life. If you are sad and tired, you emanate that energy -- likewise if you are angry or upset. Of course, when you're happy and inspired you will emanate that energy. How many of us can honestly say we spend our time happy and inspired? Yet this is where we want to focus because this is exactly the energy that attracts everything positive. When you are grateful for all that you have, you also move into an energy of abundance which attracts more of the same. This includes abundant health, abundant love and abundant joy. Wake up every morning and find just three things to be thankful for, go to bed and find three more things to be thankful for and observe as your life experience changes. Gratitude is one of the most powerful places you can move into whenever you beat up on yourself up or in any way treat yourself poorly. Give thanks for what you have, the clothes you're wearing, the air you're breathing; give thanks for your lungs that are taking those deep breaths, the heart that is pumping your blood, the legs that allow you to walk, and you will shift. Keep this up and you will find yourself prosperous, literally vibrating from the inside out. Because you are vibrating this on the inside, everything you dream of achieving will become your experience in the outer world. Just give this process a lot of gratitude and a little time, and you will see the results you truly dream of.

Please write: "I am grateful for all that I am and all that have right now, today."

_____

_____

Allow: *Dictionary Definition (v): To give permission for something to happen or somebody to do something. To let somebody or yourself have something. To let somebody or something enter and be present in a place.*

What does the word "allow" mean to you?

_____

_____

_____

_____

Defining the word "allow" in our terms meant we had to make it the last word to consider in this section of your workbook. The truth is: if you practiced everything else (wholeness, love, respect and so on) without allowing yourself, then everything else would not work. To really do this work and reap the benefits, you must first allow, or give yourself permission, to actually do it! Give yourself permission to love yourself, forgive yourself, accept yourself right here, right now, and the possibilities available to you are limitless. Struggle through this work without allowing, or giving yourself permission, and this workbook will end up unfinished somewhere amongst other things that are incomplete and unsettled. That is how important that act of allowing is.

Most of us receive the set of permissions we use all of our lives when we are children, such as: "No you can't do _____ it's not safe", or "Yes you can go to the movie, but be careful not to talk to strangers..." The silly part about this is that we haven't been kids for at least a few years, so why do we live under those same permissions now that we are all grown up? The good news is that now that we are no longer children, we can give ourselves a new set of permissions that will work so much better. Allow – give yourself a whole new set of permissions -- and enjoy the ride. Life is meant to be an amazing adventure, and you are meant to be happy and feeling great, so give yourself permission to be just that and see what happens!

Please write: "Now that I'm all grown up I give myself permission to enjoy my life, enjoy great health, enjoy great happiness. I give myself permission to love who I am. I give myself permission to be me, just as I am.''

_____
_____
_____
_____

What About Your Parents?

When it comes to saying "yes" to the body and the health you deserve and desire, we would do well to take a look at what our legacy is. Keep in mind that a legacy is what you choose it to be. You do not have to accept the way it was for the way it is or always will be. It is important to understand from where we came, because it has impacted and imprinted itself upon us and has played a role in where we find ourselves today.

What was/is your parents attitude towards health? Food? Exercise?

_____
_____
_____
_____

Without pointing a finger of accusation or blame, we simply want to understand where we came from. Let's keep in mind that our parents are people too, and they probably just did the best they could with whatever legacy they were given in their turn. They didn't realize the one thing you are learning right here and now -- that any legacy can stop at any time when we are the ones to say "no more" and transform our futures. This means that if you have children you do not have to worry any longer about impacting them in negative ways when you decide to focus on new and positive ways of being.

Were your parents athletic?

_____

_____

_____

Did they eat healthy or poorly? Did they eat junk food, fried food or health food?

_____

_____

_____

How would you describe your parents weight and health over all?

_____

_____

_____

How are you like your parents when it comes to weight and health?

_____

_____

_____

_____

Feel free to continue to explore this aspect of your history, because where you come from is a large part of who you discover yourself to be today. The point bears repeating: the past need not be a prologue to the future. You can change any part of you that you would choose to change. But in order to allow change, you must first understand where you do come from, which means reviewing the bits and pieces of your personal history that may be impacting your daily life, routine and reality right now.

The most important and final question we will ask in this section is simply this: Do you wish to continue the legacy passed to you, or do you wish to transform it?

_____

_____

_____

You are powerful and capable of anything you choose.

Your Thoughts About Food

We've more then likely come across the idea before that "We are what we eat." If we eat unhealthy foods, we will more than likely be unhealthy, and if we eat healthy foods, we will more than likely be healthy. This stands to reason and is pretty accurate; how many people do you know who eat crap and feel crappy?

We would like to take this time-tested philosophy a step further and say it this way: "Not only are you what you eat – you are what you think about what you eat!" Let us explain by sharing a simple experience. Not long ago, sitting at a table of successful business women who had gathered for a networking lunch, the waiter came around with the dessert tray, and there was a wonderful moment when every woman there pondered if she should have dessert. Some of the things they said were: "Oh, I would love to have that cheesecake, but it will just go to my hips." "I love chocolate but it doesn't love me." Then, the ever-popular, "All I have to do is look at that and I gain five pounds." And so on. As it happened, a few women did get their sinful desserts and unfortunately, that cheesecake _did_ go right to their hips and the five pounds found their way onto their bodies. Why? Because all of these women had already set the stage and told their bodies what that food was going to do to them before they even had a mouthful.

Think about it. What we say is powerful. It sets our intentions and lets the universe know what we expect, even when it comes to the food we are eating. You can imagine how hard it is to listen to someone describing their meal as "a heart attack on a plate," but people do say exactly that and then proceed to eat the food to which they have just given this terrible title.

What are some of the things you've heard people say about food they are eating, or are about to eat?

_____

_____

_____

What are some of the things you've said about food you are eating, or are about to eat?

_____

_____

_____

_____

_____

_____

_____

While this is not a "get out of jail free" card, meaning that while your thoughts and attitude about what you are putting in your body matters, this concept does not mean you now have permission to binge on sugary or fatty foods and indulge in a crap diet. Being conscious about what you are thinking about the food you are eating while you eat it can however dramatically affect your physical being, that is, when you truly bless and believe every mouthful of food you are eating is both nutritious and good for your body. Yes, even the dessert that you are enjoying - in moderation - can be feeding your body all the nutrition it requires while increasing your metabolism and allowing for weight to release! Believing wholly and completely is the key to this philosophy and when you believe what you eat is healthy, surprisingly you begin to pick healthy foods.

Realize that healthy foods, whole foods and live foods are going to be some of the best choices you can make for yourself on a daily basis. And as you enjoy your food, this concept of blessing and setting forth healthy intentions towards the foods you eat can intensify your consciousness around what you are eating and allow you to enjoy absolute nutrition and perfect energy.

So, the next time something comes across your plate that you are going to eat, remember to bless it and your body by deciding it is the best food you can put into your body at that moment. Remember and be grateful that your food is providing your body with perfect nutrition and energy, that this food is easily digested and contributing to your body becoming your most perfect and healthy body, and enjoy!

Your Thoughts About Your Body

We would be remiss to discuss the power of your thoughts and not specifically address your thoughts about your body. After all, these thoughts are the ones that set you up for success or failure.

What do you think about your body? (Please just answer as honestly as you can.)

_____

_____

_____

_____

_____

_____

_____

When was the last time you looked at yourself and told yourself what a wonderful person you are? Last night? Last week? Last month? Last year? Can you even remember the last time? For some of you, it may have been a long time ago, perhaps even decades. And for those who haven't said nice things about themselves in a _really, really, really_ long time, please understand you are not alone. Unfortunately it is more common for us not to praise ourselves then to actually think nice thoughts about who we are.

OK, so let's admit that perhaps you are not in the shape you want to be, or think you want to be. Does this make you a bad person? Who you are is not determined by what you weigh, or what you look like; who you are is determined by how you feel about yourself and who you choose to be. For example, one can choose to be a very positive and happy person. Or, one can choose to be a very sad and angry person. Likewise one can choose to participate in life and go to events, enjoy shows and the company of others, or one can stay at home alone. All are valid choices, but one set of choices may lead to more satisfying results then another set.

Who would you describe yourself to be right now?

_____

_____

_____

_____

_____

_____

_____

When you look at what you've just written about yourself, does it make you feel good? Maybe some of it does and some of it doesn't; that's fine. We want to focus on what makes us feel good, authentically. It's also fine to recognize what makes us feel bad in the process of doing this because then we know what to let go of.

Using the space below, re-write those things that made you feel good, and then add to your self-description by using your imagination to conceive of some things you would like to be. (Hint: you can pull bits and pieces from people that inspire you, even characters in a book or your favorite movie.) Just make up some stuff that, if they were truly you, would really make you feel good about who you are.

_____

_____

_____

_____

_____

_____

_____

_____

_____

_____

_____

_____

_____

_____

_____

_____

Excellent.

Check the list now and see if there is anything on it that you either want to add to or perhaps something you want to take away. Review it until you feel it's the best list you could have right now, and once you have done that, write it again on a separate piece of paper. Make many copies of this list and leave it around in places you will run into it. It's good to have one in your car, perhaps in your purse or wallet, on the bathroom mirror, by the bed and just about anywhere you know you will end up finding it throughout the day. Read it. Re-read it. Memorize it because you're reading it so much. Realize as you do this that every time you read this description of yourself, you are becoming that person. Every time you affirm positive things about who you are, you are triggering positive energy within you and all around you. Your energy will become lighter and more inspired, your outlook brighter and more positive, and your outcomes clearer, because you will see yourself as an achiever of success. You will begin to think and say good things about who you are and who you are becoming.

This is a process, but it doesn't take long for the positive shift to begin taking place. It just takes repetition. Practice does indeed make perfect.

Does this mean all the negative and unsupportive self-talk and thoughts are just going to disappear? No. But it does mean you will being to recognize those thoughts and patterns before they take over, and you will be empowered enough to change them by simply reading your self description and remembering who you are and what you are choosing. This is an extremely powerful practice.

Remember, you are an incredible and amazing person, absolutely unique in every way. In fact, you are so unique that there is no one else like you on this planet! You are a gift and you are a reflection of all things possible. It's time to start telling yourself what an incredible person you are. Think good thoughts about your body, yourself, and your life... and enjoy the results.

Radical Self-Love

Apply this everywhere in your life. We are going to apply this to your physical being for the purposes of this workbook and this applies to literally every aspect of who you are and the life you are experiencing.

The body you are currently wearing is the perfect and whole person you have always wanted to be. Would you repeat that out loud, just for the sake of personal impact. "The Body I am currently wearing is the perfect and whole person I've always wanted to be." But, you may protest, I'm overweight. I'm out of shape. I don't fit into my clothes anymore, I don't feel good, and on and on. This doesn't change the fact that the body you are in is the exact body, that is, the perfect body, in fact the only body you've got.

A radical concept? Perhaps, and consider this. Every cell, every organ, every blood vessel, lymph gland and muscle, is part of you, the whole and complete you, whether you are a larger version of your body or a smaller version. Whether you are pear-shaped, oval, round, lean, flabby, firm or any other descriptive term you would like to add, this is your body. This is the same body you will be living in when you are exactly the weight and shape you desire being.

Look at it this way: on a physical level, your body is constantly regenerating itself. New skin replaces old skin, new hair replaces old hair — everything down to your very cells is constantly replenishing. This is going to happen anyway. So ask yourself: As your thoughts intersect with your body, do you want your body to regenerate those same feelings of dissatisfaction, which continue to keep you at odds with yourself, or do you want it to regenerate itself complete with a new loving and positive energy? What do you think will be best for the most favorable results? To criticize, ridicule, put down and otherwise abuse this amazing machine known as your body, or love who you are right now?

Radial self-love means loving, forgiving and accepting yourself exactly as you are, RIGHT NOW! Radical self love means putting yourself, your body, your state of being first, yes, taking care of you first, so that you can then care for others. Have you ever sat in a plane before take off, listening to the flight attendant say that if the oxygen masks drop down while you are traveling with a young child, you need to put your own mask on before putting one on your child? This is so you can remain conscious and able to take care of others who depend on you. Now to be sure, that is an emergency scenario, and one we hope we never encounter. But the larger point remains, namely that in the art of living each day well means taking care of yourself so then your cup is overflowing, and then you will never run out no matter how many share from it.

Most importantly, radical self-love means, LOVING YOU and EVERYTHING ABOUT YOU, now.   Is this an easy thing to do? No, it certainly isn't, because life has taught us all sorts of impractical half truths about being self-less, which we can't help but define as being without your self. To perhaps put it more clearly, we are literally translating the term "self-less" to mean being less of your self, or without self. How can you show up for yourself when you are being self-less, and how can you show up for anyone else if you can't show up for yourself?

Write this down and then write it on post-its and stick them up like wallpaper: "I completely love, forgive and accept myself exactly as I am, right now."

_____

_____

_____

Say this aloud as many times as you remember. Make it your mantra and chant it; say it in the mirror directly to yourself, and one day you will find yourself being able to say it in the mirror, right into your own eyes. (When you first start doing this, don't be surprised that you end up looking at your chin, the ceiling, your forehead, etc. Just keep it up and you will end up being able to look deeply into your eyes and truly believe.)

Love all of you. Remember that the body you are in is the same body you will be in when you achieve the body you desire. Love every cell of your body right now, every aspect of your physical being.

Please write: "I love my body, my whole being and it is responding to me becoming healthier and shapelier every day. I love my body and my body releases unnecessary weight with effortless ease."

_____

_____

_____

_____

Forgive yourself. So you ate something you swore you wouldn't eat. You didn't go to exercise class yesterday. You regret saying something to someone. You didn't say the right thing, or do the right thing, etc. For whatever past or present reality, real or imagined, forgive yourself and let go. Yes, you can. Just forgive.

Please write: "I give myself permission to forgive myself and let go. I forgive. I forgive myself completely and it feels great."

_____

_____

_____

_____

Accept yourself, exactly as you are right now. Whatever you are attempting to change will change so much more easily and readily when you accept it first as it is. The energy we put into resisting something because we don't think we can accept it is wasted energy that could be used to support us in achieving the body we want and the health we deserve. Accept yourself completely, even those habits you wish to change, and you will find an inner peace that will become your inner strength because you will no longer be attempting to fix something broken. Instead, you will be excelling at allowing yourself to become better, better and better. When we see ourselves as whole, we can move towards newer and deeper variations of wholeness. When we see ourselves as broken we have nowhere to go.

Please write: "I accept who I am right now. I accept my body, I accept my ability to be anything I choose to be. I accept myself right now."

_____

_____

_____

_____

_____

Things You Can Count On
And What You Can Do About Them

<u>Resistance</u> –This can show up in many ways, both expectedly and unexpectedly. For example, it can sneak in through the act of obsessing about what another person may think of you. This can lead you down the path of resistance, especially when you are beginning to practice self-care, love and acceptance, because this is a subtle way for the old habits of self-sabotage to reinstate themselves in the form of someone else's thoughts. The best way to handle this is to recognize it when it's going on, which may take a moment, then to love, forgive and accept yourself, and get back on track with your self-care, love and acceptance. It makes sense not to beat yourself up over these things because that's actually another way resistance shows its familiar face. Could it take you days to figure out what's going on? Yes, and so what? Once you recognize something that is not serving you and let it go and get back on track, celebrate the fact that you recognized it! The time it takes you to see it will diminish each time you catch yourself and celebrate your successful return to self-care, love and acceptance.

Resistance also comes in the form of comparing yourself to someone else. No two people are the same. We are truly living works of art sculpted individually. Comparing ourselves to someone else is like comparing one sunrise to another; what is the point? We will never really know what is going on for another person. We don't have their history. We don't know their thought process, nor do we have the ability to live inside their heads or bodies, so this act of self comparison is just plain silly and serves no other purpose than to make us feel inadequate. Think of it this way; would you take a pill labeled "Make Yourself Feel Inadequate"? The next time you catch yourself comparing yourself to someone else, put the "pill" down and make a different choice. Love, forgive, accept and get back on track. Celebrate your recognition of resistance, let go and move on.

Unfortunately sometimes even the ones we love will not understand what we are doing and why we are doing it. In their own way, they will become a nay sayer — oftentimes with the best of intentions! This is one of the tougher types of resistance to recognize and face because we believe that those who love us are, or should be, supportive. We must gain the perspective that even those who love us and are a huge part of our lives have their own stories going on, and they may be making choices that are not allowing them to live a happy life. They may have settled or sold out somewhere along the way, and while they don't necessarily know that they have done this, they are viewing you through their limitations.

Love them anyway, and most importantly remember to love yourself. Love, forgive and accept you first, and it will become a natural act to do this for another, even though they may have let you down. One thing you can look forward to is that most of them will come around at some point when they see how happy you are and what you are achieving. Yes, it would be nice if they were there from the beginning, but they, like you, are also human. Love, forgive, accept and realize you do not need to defend your stand for yourself to anyone. Convincing anyone that you are a deserving and worthy person is getting caught in a conversation that may not go in a healthy direction. Recognize these little traps and let them go. Love, forgive and accept. Celebrate your ability to disengage these adversities and move on.

Then there's The Scale. Ah yes, The Bathroom Scale. It can be the biggest and fastest pitfall anyone releasing weight can encounter. This is adversity at its finest. When you are in the process of saying "yes" to the body you want and deserve, you might want to get on the scale when you start and then get on it again when you get to a size you want so you can celebrate the total pounds lost. Understand that is it best to lose body fat, and that may end up having some surprising results when it comes to weights and measures! Neither one of us actually has a scale in her house, but if you choose to get on the scale from time to time, or if a doctor recommends that you stand on a scale as part of your health regime, we want to address the fact that it may not always say what you think it should. Muscle weighs more then fat, and sometimes we are trimming down and firming up. This means that we are replacing fat with muscle and that can show up on the scales like we haven't lost weight when in fact, we have lost fat which is the most important thing we could achieve so in essence we have released weight that the scale doesn't recognize because it isn't designed to tell the difference between muscle and fat.

There are many reasons the scales may not say what we want them to, but understand that they will soon reflect all the work you are doing, so just stick with it. Maybe you can resist getting on the scale and put it away for a week or two. Focus instead on how you feel. Do you feel good after eating what you just ate? Do you have energy? We want to focus on feeling good and ultimately practicing self love. By tuning into how we feel after we eat, we can quickly learn what food serves us and what food drains us. Also, during this time you can allow yourself to relax into the process and learn to reestablish your personal body connection which will let you know if you are on track or off track.

Note; sometimes the scales don't move when they ought to be because our metabolism is a bit messed up. What messes up metabolisms? Ironically, dieting can be one of the biggest causes for screwing up our natural rhythm; hormones and/or stress can also be culprits. There are a lot of natural remedies, traditional and holistic approaches to getting your metabolism back in gear. It is not the purpose of this workbook to diagnose or recommend specific supplements, herbs or tonics. What we would like to suggest is that you leave no stone unturned and do some research. A world of information is literally at your fingertips on the internet. Consider a visit to your local herbalist, Naturopath or Compound Pharmacist. If you are lucky enough to have a China Town close by, that can be a great place to explore, ask questions and find out everything you can about what is best for you and your body.

Breakdown – Rest assured that as far as you go, you will have moments when you encounter breakdown. These are moments when you see yourself participating in habits that you know are sabotaging your overall success. This could mean going on a junk food eating binge, or choosing to lie on the couch for several days practicing old, bad habits. It could even mean putting this workbook aside, maybe even just sentences away from finishing it! All of this is fine, if you can find the place within you to allow forgiveness and acceptance. We've all heard the term "unconditional love" -- now is the time to learn what that means because it's exactly this type of self-love that will see you through any breakdown you may face.

Love, forgive and accept yourself exactly as you are. When you find yourself in breakdown mode, take a breath and understand: now that you recognize what is happening, you can start to allow yourself to explore different options and choices. This is where transformation happens.   Ask yourself what's really going on here, and listen to what starts to come up for you. The emotions and answers that emerge from this self-exploration will expose some of the deeper reasons you may be holding on to extra weight.

Breakdowns are important. They often result in breakthroughs, which is great. Realize one very important thing: it took time for you to get to where you are, and it is going to take time for you to get to where you want to be. You'll be surprised to discover that it isn't anywhere near the time you may think, but, you must give yourself permission to take the time you require in order to do whatever personal work you need in order to achieve all you desire.

Embrace the process with love and acceptance because it's not a question of "if" there will be any breakdowns – it's a question of "when" there will be one.   Give yourself permission to do what it takes to heal and be open to the process.

Please write: "I give myself permission to do what it takes and allow for whatever time I need to discover that all I require in love, forgiveness and acceptance."

_____

_____

_____

_____

_____

Addictions - We all have addictions on some level. Be it waking up to a cup of coffee or tea every morning or something a little more sinister; addictions come in all forms. A lot of folks are addicted to struggle, working really hard, not having enough or not being enough. Self-esteem or lack thereof seems to be at the heart of many addictions, and for the truly unhealthy addictions like drugs or alcohol, very poor self-esteem would be an especially dangerous and damaging culprit.

Anorexia or bulimia also fit into the fabric of addictive behavior, as both involve a force that seems to be beyond one's control. Be it starving oneself or binging and purging, both are self-depreciating behaviors that can lead to serious illness and even death. Food addicts struggle on a daily basis with just being able to eat to live and some addictive behaviors of this nature can lead to zoned out binge-eating usually of junk food and candy. There are sugar addicts and fast food junkies who try to feel better by eating only to feel worse.

The biggest challenge anyone faces around eating disorders and food addictions is that unlike other addicts who can stop using in order to get well, quitting food is not an option. Therefore, healing their relationship to food is their only real option. If you are wondering what addictive tendencies you may have, addictive behaviors are those which we know aren't healthy or good for us but we find ourselves doing anyway, even after we have promised ourselves we wouldn't.

If you are facing an addiction that is contributing to your current situation, the time has come to address it. The reality is that if you don't address it today, you will have to face it one day if there is to be any form of change. This is not meant as judgment. As you read the personal stories of both Miranda and Deborah you will find you are not alone on this path and that this work befalls all of us who choose a better way.

There are amazing programs available for just about every addiction going, so the good news is there is no shortage of help and assistance. It just takes courage to ask or to show up, and to begin to embrace the change that will literally transform your life. There is no shame in being human. You came from somewhere and have had the experiences you have had, and for those reasons you have landed where you are at this moment. This has been your personal journey, good or otherwise. The trick here is not to remain stuck in these places but to release, let go, forgive and love yourself anyway. You are not alone.

Please write: "I love, forgive and accept myself, exactly as I am, right now"

_____

_____

A Different Way to think About "Fat"!

When we are dealing with the issue of being overweight, we are dealing with an excess of fat that is settled within our bodies in all the wrong places. For the most part, this leads us to dislike our body, and to treat our body as if there is something wrong with it. Having addressed the idea that the body you are in is the same body you will be in when you are your ideal shape, we now want to share with you a rather interesting way to view fat. In many ways, this is a very accurate description of what fat may indeed really be. We would like you to consider that fat is, in its own way, a parasite.

A parasite as represented in the dictionary is "a living organism that lives on a larger host organism in a way that harms or is of no advantage to the host." Let's consider this for a moment. Fat is a layer of cells that lives under the skin and in the case of being over weight; it is a layer of cells that lives under the skin in excess. It does not contribute to its host in any way that is positive; in fact, it drains the host – your body – of energy, health and happiness. It is emotionally hard to be heavy. It is physically draining to carry around extra weight, as that weight can place undue wear on joints and organs. This would be in alignment with the nature of a parasite – it harms or is of no advantage to its host.

A parasite demands feeding. Fat doesn't want to eat complex foods, like whole foods, live foods or health foods that actually take energy and time to digest. Fat is much happier when it's being fed junk foods, fast foods and sugar in mass quantities. These are all things that it can digest without effort and get maximum bang for the buck. Many junk foods will leave someone on a temporary high after they've been eaten, only to then crash, which makes the host want to have more of the same bad, fatty and sugar-filled things in pursuit of that temporary high. It is a vicious roller coaster. Consider this very seriously for the moment: when you participate in a diet of this nature, you are not feeding your body, your emotional or mental well-being. You are feeding the fat. You are feeding dysfunction, and the end result is a body that feels bad and is out of shape.

On a personal level, when you can begin to separate your identity from the fat you want to release, you become stronger than your cravings, stronger then your old bad habits, and stronger than your emotional baggage. When you can see the "you" that is inside, separate from the weight and the fat, then you are seeing the new, slimmer, lighter or shapelier "you" -- and this is who you begin to feed and take care of. It's a lot easier to say "no" to temptation when you are able to see the choice before you as feeding a parasite versus feeding your body and your health.

One final thought on this subject is that it is more important to lose the fat than it is to lose weight. If you are losing muscle but keeping the fat this is not healthy nor will it last. Yes, it can take more time to release fat versus simply doing the fad diet to drop a few pounds. But that is precisely the point when the pounds you drop quickly come back, and unfortunately when we eat away at our muscle, we usually end up gaining more fat back. Deny the parasite. Feed your body good foods and enjoy amazing results.

What it FEELS like to Succeed and Feel Great

A question was asked by a friend who helped to review this workbook while it was in the creative process which was; "What is it like when you are successful with this, what does it feel like"? It was such an excellent question! So often we work on something but are so used to it being hard and challenging, or we are just so used to feeling bad, that we don't know what it would mean to experience the shift to feeling good and successful.

When we actually begin to treat ourselves better we naturally start feeling better, and the more we practice this experience the greater the good feeling gets. What could this feel like? It's like an inner peace, a deep calm that seems to wash over you and wash away anxiety and stress. It's like arriving at a holiday destination you've always wanted to go to but have never been before. Imagine stepping into a beautiful environment that stimulates your senses in wonderful ways. It's the most incredible place of inner contentment and joy that comes from within you and requires no outside stimulants of any kind; in fact, no stimulant of any kind will ever get you to this place. No food, ride, sport, man, woman, nor any external force can make you feel this way. It comes from within like the sun rising on a perfect day.

At first it may not be that noticeable. It just may be that you are more inclined to smile because you feel like it. It may be that you start waking up in a good mood and then you might start looking forward to your day. You may have a little bounce in your step, or just feel like doing something a little different because it sounds like fun.

For some, feeling good means the heaviness that seems to be part of your being somehow disappears. This can happen in stages, meaning you will feel lighter over time until you realize you feel light all the time. Emotionally, there will be less turmoil and drama; physically, there will be less discomfort, fatigue, aches and pains; mentally, there will be less confusion and less feeling overwhelmed. This means that emotionally, you will feel more contented (happy with what you have and with what's happening around you), more connected and more in charge. Physically, you will feel more energy, better health, rested and more able to function in comfort. Mentally, you will be clearer and more able to focus and achieve things thus allowing for success.

When you know you are on track, you will feel your energy going up and be more inspired overall. Yes, this does mean that it is wise to do things that inspire you while reconsidering and even letting go those things that frustrate or disenchant you. When you are on track you start to have creative thoughts or spontaneous ideas, and you start to see possibilities and solutions where only problems and challenges used to be. This doesn't all happen at once (although it could), and it doesn't happen over night (although we like to be open to it happening as quickly as possible)! And you will have days where the "old" stuff seems to surface. This does mean that over time, you will have more good in your life overall, and when the bad stuff does appear momentarily, you will see it clearly for what it is and let it roll off you versus allowing it to distract you.

The truth is, for as much as we are attempting to illustrate what feeling good and feeling success can be like, it is unique to every individual, so the best gauge may simply be, how do you feel right this moment? When you are on track you will always feel more positive, even if it is by a fraction of a hair, and the more you recognize this unfolding in your life, the more you will attract it. A great example would be this: Go to a mirror and take this book with you. Once in front of the mirror put on your best frown -- you know, that furrowed brow scowl that distorted your whole face. Look at yourself frowning in the mirror and ask, how does this feel? Write down your answers.

How does this feel:

_____

_____

Now look back at the mirror and instead of frowning, smile. Give that BIG smile, that silly, goofy smile that shows all your teeth. Take a good look and ask yourself, how does this feel? Write down your answers. (It may take a moment to feel the shift.)

How does this feel:

_____

_____

Now compare notes. Feeling good and successful feels like you smiling the biggest smile you can imagine from the inside out. (Remember, no matter what the situation, you can always choose to smile – it increases your face value!)

The Final – and Life Long – Exercise of Self Reinvention;
How to Say YES to the Body You Want.
(You will need a notebook, or pad of paper for this.)

This process would be far from complete if this piece were not here for you to work through, develop and mold as your heart guides you. Notice we did not say your head. With specific intention, we left this process in the very capable hands of your heart, your feeling and emotions. Based on the philosophy in this workbook, you must first heal before you are able to move on, or in this case, self reinvent -- and that involves your emotions and feelings first and foremost. Before you think about who you want to be, how you want to be, what your ideal body is, make sure you FEEL about who you want to be, how you want to be and what your ideal body is! Your internal emotional guidance system is tried, true and absolutely accurate when you allow it to be. Trust the process and realize that this IS doing it differently and that means, different results.

First, define what you want: This is quite simple to do when you follow these next steps. Keep in mind that most everybody knows what they don't want. In fact if you ask someone what they want they might have an item or two on their list but for the most part the answer they will give will start with; "Well, I don't want..... and I really don't want... and I certainly don't want....... Either!" This doesn't work when it comes to attracting what you want because what you are focused on is what you don't want, and that's what you get.

The nervous system cannot "not process." Put another way, while you are alive, your nervous system is constantly moving towards something, and that something is whatever you are focused on. It doesn't understand "don't," "not" or "no", so every time you say, think or debate about what you don't want, all you have to do to is remove the "don't," "not" or "no" from the sentence and that will clearly reveal what you are actually focused on. For example if you are focused on how much you don't want to be hungry right now, all you have to do is remove the don't to reveal the truth of what you are actually focused on which is, how much you want to be hungry right now! Your nervous system is moving towards whatever you place in front of it. So, if all you are thinking of is what you don't want, that is all you can have because it's the only thing in front of you. The trick is to identify what you <u>do</u> want so you can begin to focus on that; then your nervous system will move towards what you do want and in time, you will receive exactly that.   For example borrowing from the above analogy if you were to move towards what you want, you would be focused on how satisfied you are right now and how good you feel.

Knowing what you don't want is the place to start in this exercise so it's fine if that's all you know in the moment.

<u>The Action Steps</u>: Take a blank piece of paper, or page in your notebook. Draw a line vertically down the center of the page, creating two columns, and then put the title "What I Don't Want" on the left hand column and the title "What I Do Want" on the right hand column.   Next, without too much effort or thought, simply start to write down what you don't

want anymore around your life, health, weight and whatever comes up. Just keep writing until you are done. Yes, this can take time and paper! Keep going, making sure to create those same two columns on every page as you go. When you are done, take a break.

Ok... Now comes the fun part. Go back to the top of you left column and start going down your "Don't Want" list one item at a time. As you read the "Don't Want" out loud, ask yourself this question; "What would I have if I didn't have that?" Write the answers down in the right hand column, that is, your "Do Want" column. Once you have transformed a "don't want" into a "do want," scratch out the "don't want" and move on. Do this for each item on your list. Once again, this will take time but it's worth the energy.

Once you have completed your whole list you may want to rewrite your wants so they are clear and contained as their own list. Finally, the last part of this exercise is as follows. When your want list is complete, go back and read it one item at a time, and ask the last question; "If I had this right now, who would I be". This question is all about connecting to the feeling of having what you want, right here and right now. Write out your answers, as you are now creating a treasure map that is filled with who you choose to be, and who you are becoming. Keep these two lists close by; in fact make copies of them so you can have easy access to them and read them OFTEN! Whenever things start to feel in any way bad or uncomfortable, just refer to your list and ask if you are in alignment with what you want and who you are being. If the answer is "no", you simply decide what path you are going to take — your "don't wants", or your "do wants" — and take the appropriate action. It sure makes transformation easy when you know where you are going.

This exercise is great for defining anything you want in any area of your life. Use it often.

The Next Level of Clarity

It has already been said in a few ways in this workbook that what we focus on, feel, believe, dwell on or otherwise give our energies to is what we receive. If we feel bad about ourselves we tend to have things happen to us that cultivate feeling bad. Likewise, if we feel good about ourselves we tend to have things happen to us that cultivate feeling good. It's would appear to be obvious that if you have gone this far with this workbook then you are looking to feel good, and while it may seem like a daunting task, feeling good can be affirmed into your life with this simple and direct statement.

Repeat this aloud: "I completely love, forgive and accept myself, exactly as I am."

This is an affirming statement of transformation; in fact we recommend it become your mantra. It engages every aspect of personal change by inviting pure love, unconditional forgiveness, and absolute acceptance of the most valuable and important treasure you possess, which is yourself.

Any resistance that comes up around this statement is merely your road map to and through healing that is required. The fastest way we know of to release and move through resistance is to use your journal and allow yourself to write about whatever is coming up. No editing; just go for it. Once you feel you have spewed out all your thoughts, feelings and emotions, review it. Pretend you are in a movie theater and what you are reviewing is playing on the screen in front of you. This is a great way to get a little perspective and not be triggered by what you are reviewing. As you are going through what you have written, stop periodically and ask yourself: "Is this on track and in alignment with what I am wanting? Also, "Does this feel good?" And finally, "Is this really true?" Write down your answers and explore them in the same way until you have moved through the resistance by painting a new picture based on what you want, feeling good, and the truth of who you are becoming.

If you find you have pages of stuff you don't want to hang on to once you have completed this process, you can tear them out and burn them or shred them, and you can consider this final step a symbolic step to freedom!

Sometimes we find we have some extremely deep issues that are not going to just resolve in this process quickly. This doesn't mean the process won't work for you; it just means that this may be a time to consider working with someone who can assist you in the release and healing of these particular issues. Please know you have all of our personal contact information; we are here to serve you and help you to heal. Or perhaps there is someone you know of who you feel guided to work with. The point is: if you find that you are requiring guidance, assistance and/or clarity to help you move through your past and become complete with it, listen to that inner voice and work with someone. It will speed up the process and give you tremendous and valuable results.

Please write on a separate piece of paper and then on as many post-its as you dare: "I completely love, forgive and accept myself exactly as I am."

Put these post-its everywhere. In the car, on your person (purse or wallet) on the fridge, by the bed, in your office, on your bathroom mirror and everywhere else you can think of. Say it out loud, say it to yourself, whisper it, yell it and sing it. Laugh your way through it, cry your way through it, smile your way through it and speak it as often as you can. As the famous commercial would say "Just DO IT!"

Practicing Gratitude

To be grateful is to generate a vibration of abundance. To be grateful is to realize how blessed we are. To be grateful is the fastest way to shift energy from a place of negative vibration — perhaps attracting things we don't want — to a positive one. A positive vibration will support positive behaviors and attract positive situations. An attitude of gratitude is the most powerful mindset we can have.

In keeping with daily practices that are aligning you with the body and health you want, create a gratitude list. Just write out everything you've got to be grateful for, right here and right now on this list. You can add to it as often and as much as you like; in fact, as you start this process you may find only a few things, which is perfect, but as you continue, you may discover more and more things to be grateful for, and that is the point and purpose of this exercise.

This gratitude list is a general list, so it can look like the following:

"I'm so grateful for my home, my appliances, my car, the food on my table, the heat and running water, the view out my window, my dog, my cat, for every breath I take and for another day. "

Of course it can be anything you choose; that is just and example, your list can include people, relationships, work, income increasing daily, and all that good stuff.

Another additional and important thing you can do with your gratitude list is to also practice that law of attraction by giving thanks for things you are attracting right now. This is a slightly more advanced way to use your gratitude list and should not replace thanks for the here and now but rather be added to it.

Let's say you are clear that you want something specific to happen in your life, like the release of weight. Well one of the things you can add to your gratitude list is exactly that, and you might write it this way:

"I'm so grateful for the healthy and effortless release of weight off of my body. I look great, feel great and I am vital and healthy."

Another example may be that you want a happy and loving relationship in your life with a significant other, so you may write:

"I'm so grateful for this amazing, loving and happy relationship I'm sharing with my wonderful mate".

Once again, this should not replace those things you are grateful for in the here and now, but rather this aspect of your gratitude list should be "in addition to."

Once you have written your gratitude list, which we understand is always a work in progress, make a commitment to read it out loud at least once a day. When you read this list, please understand that it's important to truly feel grateful. Perhaps you can read it when you wake-up and/or when you go to bed. Our best suggestion is that you read it on both occasions, upon arising and then retiring, so that your day starts and ends with this magnificent energy. To get started, once a day may be more doable for you. What you will notice is that your attitude and energy will shift every time you speak out loud all the amazing things you feel grateful for. What a way to start — and finish — each day!

The last part of this gratitude exercise is a little more spur of the moment and requires your focus in a spontaneous way every day. This is something we recommend you start at the beginning of your day and then remind yourself of throughout the whole day. Do this part after you have reviewed and read your gratitude list because you will be in the perfect place for it.

Every morning discover three things about yourself that you are grateful for and write them down on a post-it. Carry that post-it with you everywhere and check in with it often, reading and re reading (aloud when you are able) those three things all day long. Maybe it's that you have great eyes, amazing skin, that you are smart, organized, give great hugs, like to laugh, have a unique style, that you can speak or hear, or that you have a loving heart. Maybe it's that you are reliable, trustworthy or can be counted on. Maybe you're a fantastic cook, or have a great eye and an appreciation for art. You name it! In fact, name three every day and then focus on them throughout the day.

Some of the things you come up with may be redundant but that's fine -- just a long as you find three things every day about yourself that you are grateful for. This may seem like a task at first, but the more you do it, the easier it gets. What this exercise is all about is exploring the magnificence of you. This simple gesture will put you in touch with things about you that you may take for granted or just not acknowledge as wonderful when they truly are. Likewise, the more you begin to acknowledge yourself, the more you discover how great you are and the more inclined you are to take better and better care of you.

If you get stuck, think about the things you admire in others and ask yourself if you have any of them too. We usually have the qualities or at least the capacity for those things we admire most in others or we wouldn't be attracted to them. If your list reads like this: "I'm grateful for the color of my eyes, that I have long fingernails and that I love my dog" that is a perfect list.

Focus on the good and more good will come. Have fun and above all be grateful.

Your Ideal Body

This is an invitation to sit quietly, breath deeply and envision what your ideal body feels like. This is a practice that will take some time to really understand and it is absolutely valuable to imagine yourself living in your ideal body right now because it sends every cell, every molecule, a message that then moves every cell and molecule of your being towards the manifestation of your ideal body.

Yes, knowing how much weight you are choosing to release is part of this practice, so when you start your visualization, you can see the smaller body and shape. In order to become emotionally invested, it is very important to also feel what it is like to live inside that body you are envisioning. It is those things that we become emotionally invested in that manifest the fastest, so why not become lovingly, emotionally invested in you ideal body?

A tool that will help you along this path – should you choose to use it – is a vision board that could have pictures of certain rewards you will give yourself when you reach certain targets along your journey. Your vision board could include pictures of new outfits you are going shopping for, perhaps a spa where you will spoil yourself along the way, maybe even a tropical vacation. It's important to put things on your path that inspire you and also reward your actions as you go forward. Remember that life is a journey; it's not just about arriving at the next destination, so decide to fill your journey with fun stops along the way.

Another important image you can work with on your vision board is your own body image. You can place on your vision board several images of what you feel are healthy and happy bodies so your mind can begin to see your body in the same way. Be aware that those stick figure, high fashion bodies are not what we are aiming for -- we are aiming for healthy bodies that we feel good in, and everyone's body is different. Your ideal size is going to be what looks good on you, not what looks good on someone else. If you really want to have fun, draw pictures of yourself along the path, releasing weight and ultimately being the weight and body shape you see as your ideal.

Whether you choose to use a vision board or not, remember that the practice of visioning (which is basically a focused meditation) will put you in touch with how it feels from the inside out to be living in what you consider your ideal body. "Ideal" in this sense means, healthy, vibrant, strong and vital. Breathe deep and envision feeling healthy, vibrant, strong and vital. Just the act of deep breathing alone will center and invigorate you. Imaging how it feels to be where you are headed is a key element to achieving the body you want, so make the commitment to spend time on this every day, or at the very least every other day. The more you practice this, the more you will get into the feeling of it and the more you feel it, the faster it will attract and become real in your life.

This process of visualizing and then emotionally engaging, or feeling what it feels like to be where you are headed is a tried and true method recommended by every self growth or personal development teaching we have ever come across -- because it works. Feel free to use this practice in any area of your life. Remember: what you become emotionally invested in will manifest the fastest.

Your Ideal Life

Although we have focused this workbook on your physical being, you may have noticed references to the fact that each practice we are offering also can apply to any and every area of your life, as is reflected in other teachings, workshops and books or workbooks we offer and are creating. In order to bring this point home and in order to know we have touched on everything that could contribute to your hanging on to things you no longer want (mainly extra weight), it's important to realize that living a life you are truly happy with is key to the ultimate success of manifesting your ideal anything!

This touches on all aspects of your daily existence including relationships and career choices. You and only you know if you are happy in these areas, and as you work through each step of this workbook you will also realize how important these things are to your eventual and permanent success. Learning to thrive inside a healthy and happy body, but living in a day to day reality of going into a work situation you can't stand will not balance out. While you may indeed succeed with achieving your ideal body, you will probably end up falling back into bad habits to compensate for unhappiness you may be experiencing in your job, career or relationship. (Often in relationships when we become happy within ourselves our relationships excel in extremely positive ways.)

As you process through your personal wants and desires, be sure to take a moment to look at the bigger picture. We aren't suggesting you run out and make any sudden or radical shifts; just know that attention will eventually be required in any area of your life that isn't giving you what you deserve, namely health, happiness and prosperity. (Keep in mind that prosperity means many things to many people.) Be kind, loving and gentle every step of the way, and you will soon discover a kind, loving and gentle world filled with harmony and joy.

A Word about Adversity

Adversity comes in every shape and size. It can come from your family, your spouse or life partner; it can be your friends, it can even be a stranger questioning and challenging your desire to change. The confusing part about all this is that, for the most part, these other people actually mean well. They have good intentions and are trying to "protect" you. However, they have their own issues, fears and limitations, and they are projecting those in your direction in the name of concern for your well-being.

In most cases, this does not add up to a supportive environment. Loved ones can easily diminish confidence without saying much more then a few sentences. Please understand that "They know not what they do" and accept it all for what it is -- their "stuff" -- and do whatever you must do to build up and maintain your confidence. Above all else, stay your path. No one else has the right to limit, question or discourage you from making changes and going for your dreams.

When you learn to accept adversity without giving it a whole lot of meaning or credence, you soon find yourself being able to smile in the face of it and just let it go. Understand as well that when you change anything in your life, from your physical appearance to your career path, and you start to live life on your terms, it can be a direct confrontation to the lives others are living. Sometimes people, even those closest to us, do not want their status quo stirred up in any way as they are firmly ensconced in their comfort zones, even if their comfort zone is an unhealthy one. Let go and allow them to be who they are. Realize that as you manifest the body you want and the health you deserve, and as you make any other positive changes in your life, you are quietly and directly becoming a beacon of possibility to everyone around you. Shine bright!

Beyond Will Power

It takes determination to make changes in your life. Will power can be used from time to time as a tool, but it alone will not, nor will it ever, allow you to arrive at your destination. If your will power happens to be strong enough to get you to your destination, it will burn out eventually, and you will be back in the vicinity of where you started. So, let's decide right now to get in touch with our inspiration and allow that force to drive us forward.

"How do I do this?" you may ask, and the answer is a little different for everyone, because everyone is a little different. What you have already covered in this workbook has set the stage for you to reveal your point of inspiration to yourself. To further understand what we mean by this, enjoy the following story.

The Story of Joe

Once upon a time, maybe about a day or so ago, in a land just around the corner, there lived a man named Joe. Joe lived a relatively simple life in his 1200 square foot white, walled, two bedroom house with his wife of four years, Amy. Amy was the love of Joe's life and he thanked God daily for the day they met.

As it turned out, on this day Joe had even more to be thankful for because Amy had just found out that she was expecting! Everything on the outside seemed to be going Joe's way except that Joe was, by his doctor's definition, grossly overweight. If he didn't do something about it, his health was at serious risk.

Joe had had a weight problem most of his life, but with all the pressures of his job, the rising cost of living, and the added little extras that came with owning a 1200 square foot white walled two bedroom house, Joe's weight had skyrocketed to the highest it had ever been over the last few years. Amy worried about Joe because he just seemed too busy to worry about himself and now with a baby coming she wondered if he could handle the extra stress. Joe was so excited about the coming arrival of his child, he decided he was finally going to do something about all the extra weight he had gained. As it was, he was out of breath climbing his front stairs, and he knew he needed to be in a lot better shape to keep up with a baby. So, Joe woke up the next morning with a whole new attitude. He decided he was going to eat right, exercise, and slowly but surely, get himself back in shape. With this new attitude, he headed out into his day. But even though he walked up a flight of stairs instead of taking the elevator and ate a healthy and light lunch, his new attitude couldn't hold back the pressures of the day. By the time Joe headed for home, he was feeling exhausted and overwhelmed.

Joe slowly edged his way home in rush hour traffic only to find himself stopped right in front of his favorite ice cream shop. He knew he had decided to make changes, but in the midst of all the stress of the day, he decided that since he was so large already, what difference would one more ice cream make? So, he pulled his car over and went into the ice cream shop.

After Joe had eaten his double fudge and banana, he felt ashamed of himself. He felt like a failure because he had sworn he was changing his ways. So, he made up his mind *that tomorrow would be the day. Home he went, feeling tired and defeated.*

The End?

What happened to Joe? He had all the best intentions, and he knew more or less what to do in order to make changes for his health. But he relied on his will power, and after a long day, his will power tired out and his old habits won. The end result left him feeling pretty low. What were the odds of him succeeding the next day, if he took the same approach? Slim to none.

How could Joe do this differently?

The Story of Joe Revisited

Once upon a time....

When Joe heard about the baby he was so excited at the idea of being a parent, he suddenly felt the need to get very real with himself. Joe knew he got winded climbing up his front steps and he also knew it took a lot of energy to keep up with a baby. He thought about the health risks he was living with from day to day and realized that if he didn't do something, his child could grow up without a dad.

This made Joe very sad and then a little mad. Joe knew he wanted to be there for his children. He wanted to play with them at the park, put them on his shoulders and take them for rides. He knew that he wanted to be there for their first step, their first word, their first day of school, their graduation and their wedding day. Joe knew that now was the time to start doing things differently so he could lose the weight and be that healthy, happy dad his child deserved.

The next morning Joe woke up with a certainty he had never felt before. He thought about the future and made choices all day long that supported that vision. He climbed stairs instead of taking the elevator. He ate healthier meals and even though the stress of the day often overwhelmed him, he handled it that best way he could. On the way home in the stop-and-go traffic of rush hour, Joe happened to notice the colorful neon sign of his favorite Ice Cream Shop calling to him. At first he thought, "Why not?", but as soon as those words crossed his mind another more powerful thought took over -- the thought of his future children and all the things he wanted to do with them. Inch by inch he drove past the ice cream shop and went home where he hugged his wife and shared with her his commitment to their future.

The End
(But we think it's really the Beginning!)

Do you understand the impact of this story and how it plays out in Joe's failure or success? The first time around, Joe knew he had to do something differently, but in the end it all felt so overwhelming. In that mindset, it seemed reasonable to ask, "What difference does one more ice cream make?"

The second time through Joe not only knew he had to make a change, he got in touch with why he wanted to make that change. The more he got into what he was doing it all for, the more inspired and committed he became until, when faced with the same question, to eat the ice cream of not to eat the ice cream, he chose not to, because what he was doing and why he was doing it were that important and inspiring to him.

That is how you do it!

Find the point of your inspiration that will indeed feed your commitment and be there for you whenever you need it because it's so worth it. Maybe it's your family and/or loved ones. Maybe it's a special event you really want to attend, or a trip you've always wanted to take. Whatever the reason, find your point of inspiration and go for it! It will carry you when will power fades and temptation looms. Imagine being strong, fit and healthy. Imagine enjoying life, enjoying your dreams and living them out.

So, what is happening in your life today that is inspiring you to make a change? Write down the reasons you deserve to be healthy, release weight or maintain a healthy weight, and enjoy your future. Explore everything and dream big!

_____

_____

_____

_____

_____

_____

_____

_____

_____

_____

_____

_____

_____

_____

_____

_____

_____

_____

_____

Great! Read this often and if you choose, create a dream board with things on it that remind you of your reasons for making a change in your life today. You absolutely deserve to be happy, healthy and prosperous. Spread your wings and let inspiration be the wind beneath them.

Affirmations for "Saying Yes to the Body You Want"

Affirmations are a very powerful reinforcement of success. When used correctly, affirmations can assist you in clearly and quickly shifting your vibration to attract those new and positive things which will let you live a life filled with health, happiness and prosperity. Each time you repeat a positive affirmation, it is you saying "yes" to the body you want. Say each of the affirmations below and pay attention to how you feel when you say them. If you notice your energy going up and a general good feeling about you when you say a particular affirmation, this is a good one for you to use right now. If you notice your energy becoming tense or a tightness in your belly or your throat, that particular affirmation is too confrontational to your subconscious right now, and a modification is recommended.

We will use the first affirmation as an example: "I am open to change." If this feels good when you say it, you are on track. But if you sense tension -- perhaps your throat got tight or you coughed -- then right now "I am open to change" is triggering something that is not being seen as good in this moment. As you continue to do this work, that will change. In the meantime, you want to consider creating an affirmation that will work for you based on the same idea. Sometimes the simplest way to embrace a new idea is to just say the key word. So "I am open to change" becomes "change". The simple repetition of that word invites in the vibration, but is non-confrontational because you are not directly connecting your action or yourself to it. After a while you can add something like, "I am in the process change" and finally you will end up with "I am open to change." This will resonate and feel great.

Please pick three or four affirmations that talk to you right now, say them out loud and repeat often – whenever and wherever you can - for the next seven days. Then come back and pick three or four different ones and work with them for the next seven days and so on and so forth whenever and wherever you can. (Remember if you have any resistance, try the affirmation in different ways, like it has been illustrated above, and make modifications where needed.)

"I am open to change."

"My love for myself changes for the good."

"I feel open to change and only good comes to me."

"I allow myself to be in a loving flow."

"I treat my body with respect and it loves me back."

"I am open to experience myself with love and
I accept myself for who I am ."

"To flow with good in my heart means to
flow with love in my body."

"My body changes with the love I have for it and
it shows it and it expresses it."

"I appreciate every cell in my body as it supports
my expression of who I am."

"I love me."

"I am enjoying every day."

"I love my body."

"I love myself."

"I'm doing all the right things right now."

*"Today is a wonderful day full of blessings and
I am grateful."*

*"Everyday in everyway I'm getting better,
better and better."*

Affirmations are meant to be empowering, so have fun with them and even consider writing your own. You can also use a small tape recorder and read your affirmations into it and then play them back throughout the day. This is a great way to hear your voice saying positive and empowering things to you while you're in the car or before you go to sleep. What a great way to start and end your day!

A Commitment to the Self

The most important part of this whole process is the ability to commit to yourself and stay the course. This does not mean that you never waver, nor does it mean that you do it all perfectly all the time. We are human. We will progress each day at a time, and whether we fall off the path or stay on it, we love ourselves anyway and make whatever minor correction required to put us firmly back on the path of our desire, which is this case is saying yes to the body you want. To put it another way, we all screw up and SO WHAT! The most important thing is how you decide to react to yourself in the face of this, and either support or negate your path via your reaction.

We hereby give you permission to stumble, to fall into old habits from time to time, and to not get it "right"! We further give you permission to pick yourself up and gently brush yourself off, to recognize old habits and lovingly make a different choice. We give you permission to love, forgive, and accept yourself anytime you think you've got it "wrong," thereby giving yourself permission to make whatever choice feels good to you. Perfection is whatever you are doing right now, no more and no less. Isn't that great?

In making a commitment to yourself, what you are really doing is deciding here and now that you are truly worth whatever effort it takes to get you living inside the life in which you are happiest and healthiest. You are deciding that once you commit to loving yourself, forgiving yourself and accepting yourself, and once you commit to showing up on a daily basis for yourself, it's only a matter of time before you see exciting and affirming results. Will there be bumps in the road? Yes, and that's why you have this workbook to refer to and work through, as many times as you require, in order to keep you grounded and on target.

* * *

Are there more options for you to take advantage of — if you choose — that will further assist you on your path? Absolutely! Before we complete this workbook we wanted to inform you of some other supportive options available to you should you desire.

We have designed a Tele-Seminar that is a companion workshop to this workbook. It goes in greater depth and beyond every issue we have addressed in these pages. This is not designed to replace the value of this workbook and is not necessary to your success; rather, it will enhance your experience, provide your results at a faster pace, and connect you to a community who are all on a similar journey of healing, release and success. Contact us at: **800 345 9688**

Extension 0330 for further information, a list of upcoming dates, and to sign up.

Due to the nature of this interactive workshop, seating is limited.

You can also log on to:
http://www.just-say-yes-international.com and go to "Workshops & Workbooks".

We also offer training in the "YES Method" for the purpose of Life Coach certification. Contact us at: 800 345 9688 Extension 1329 for further information, training schedules and to enroll go to or log on to:
http://www.just-say-yes-international.com and go to "YES Method / Coaching".

Other resources we found to have great value include: Louise Hay's book, "You Can Heal Your Life," and Dr. Joseph Murphy's "The Power of the Subconscious Mind". For more resources please log on to: http://www.just-say-yes-international.com and go to "Links".

Deborah and Miranda are also available for individual consultation, private coaching, visioning and more. Please contact us at: **800 345 9688 extension 0333** for further information and to schedule your free "getting to know you" mini session.

* * *

That said, let's get on with finalizing your commitment to yourself, your body, your health and your life. **Please sign and date the following statement:**

I _____ do joyously commit to love, forgive and accept myself today and every day for where I am in this very moment. I commit to spending time on me, nurturing, healing and releasing myself and my body from old hurts, judgments and pain. I commit to taking care of my body and myself, because I understand that I am worth it. I commit to saying "yes" to the body I want, and I commit to saying "yes" to the life I want because I understand – and I am understanding a little more every day -- that I do deserve this. I commit to allowing myself to grow and supporting myself in this work every day to the best of my ability.

I commit to taking actions on a daily basis, be they large or small, that are all about my journey and my health, happiness and prosperity.

Signed:_____

Dated:_____

Amazing work, we salute you.

We suggest that you consider writing this out "as is" and putting a couple copies up to remind you of your commitment to yourself, your body and your health.

Completion

Congratulations, you've made it to this moment; what now lies in front of you is the rest of your life. The best part is that whatever you did yesterday, last week, last month or last year, does not matter. In fact, what you did an hour ago no longer matters because it is the past! Let the past be the past! Embrace a future of your choosing and enjoy the ride!

Can you really have the body you want? Absolutely – YES.

Remember it takes time to allow for change, and for healthy weight loss and/or a healthy body image to emerge. (Imagine a cocoon laying quiet and dormant through the season until one day a beautiful butterfly emerges.) Time is the answer when it comes to change on this level, and allowing yourself the time it takes to embrace a healthy, happy and permanent change is one of the best gifts you will ever give yourself. This change is a life-long reality and when you treat it as a process — one day at a time — you can expect to see amazing results that remain yours forever.

When you look at fashion magazines or advertisements in any media that use women to sell, remember that those women are air brushed, body taped, pushed up and pulled back. They are back lit, front lit, side lit and all the way around made to look beyond human. Their career choice is one that focuses on being a specific body type that is not always healthy and does not last. (Just a quick aside: It has been tabulated that A-List celebrities spend upwards of $150,000 a year on procedures, trainers etc., to look the way they do. I imagine we could all look like them with that kind of budget in hand!) This is not the measuring stick to use when you are creating your healthy happy body, so just enjoy the fashion magazines and all other media for what they are -- a fantasy image -- and allow yourself to manifest a healthy, shapely and perfect body because that is what you deserve.

And so, our final words are "LOVE THYSELF." You are a most precious gift to be treasured, nurtured and celebrated. May you be all you dream with effortless ease and always in grace.

About the Authors

Miranda Sullivan and **Deborah Bishop** have both used the principles in this book to transform their lives in powerful ways. Here is a part of their stories.

Miranda's Story (Weight Loss)

The very first time I had an issue with my weight was in 6th grade. That summer I decided I wanted to be thinner because I had put on ten pounds, so I chose to begin a self-imposed diet. The will power kicked in and it worked. But of course, it wasn't at all a solution to the struggles I would wage for many years over gaining and losing weight.

I became pregnant while I was still a Teenager that, of course, was another emotional experience. After I had my Son, I was somewhere between ten to fifteen pounds overweight and my roller coaster had begun its slow but treacherous climb. With each seemingly failed relationship I'd cut back on my eating and lose weight, trying to make myself feel good again. I was heavy when I did get married, and when I saw my marriage failing I again focused on my weight to make myself feel better. I decided to drink some stuff and lost 4 dress sizes in 3 months and allowed that to make me think I was OK. Then, when it seemed I finally had control over my weight and health, my financial life went into the toilet. The ongoing drama I was living on a daily basis was making me crazy.

The death of my 22 year-old Son was an emotional devastation more than I could bear, and after a few years, I found myself wearing a size 18 and weighing over 200 pounds. The weight I swore I would never get to, just goes to show, you get what you focus on!

The pivotal moment for me came the day I realized that nothing was working, personally or financially. In fact I was in enough pain to simply say "enough," and that's when life changed for me. I started to figure out that I had a lot of work to do around healing, and I decided I was worth just enough to start down this road and reclaim my life.

The steps illustrated in this book were all part of the journey of spirituality and self-respect that I took to release the weight I had. In about 1½ years, while eating right and being active, I lost over 90 pounds and went down to a size seven. Interestingly enough, that was the same weight I was when I was in 6th grade! Ultimately I have landed on being a size eight because that's what feels good and healthy to me. I have remained a size eight for quite some time now and know I will continue to do so because I am happy from within.

Where do our challenges with body image and weight start? For some of you, it was something bad that happened in your life; for others it was simply an ordinary influence, perhaps a behavior passed down from Mom or Dad. Things affect us as children, and we don't know how to let go of the emotions around those events. As adults, we all deserve to release whatever is holding us back so we can move on to live happy, healthy, and prosperous lives.

Thank you for letting me share my story with you.

Deborah's Story (Anorexia)

My journey involved not weight gain but self-starvation, otherwise known as Anorexia. This is a debilitating condition that robs the body of health and vitality because as one self-starves, the body literally starts to strip mine its own resources. To this day I still deal with certain realities because I spent so many years not giving my body what it needed.

The roots of this condition were a series of events that happened in my childhood over which I had no control. I ended up feeling I was bad, damaged, and unworthy. I was terrified that I was unable to stop anything from happening in my life, and I thought that deciding whether to eat or not to eat was the only thing I could control -- so I stopped eating.

I started this behavior when I was ten. Initially, I was "chubby" as a kid and teased because of it. It turned out I wasn't so much chubby as I was short; I ended up growing three inches and as a result became bone thin. It was then that I started to exercise constantly; I was up to 300 sit-ups done in bed before I would go to sleep— and not eat.

Throughout my teens I was approximately 85 pounds. I look at pictures of myself then and it distresses me to think that at that time, I thought I looked great. I was also quite sick and spent much of my time as a teenager in hospitals with a chronic and life-threatening condition I can now see was partially caused by my immune system being literally wasted due to the anorexia. It was after several surgeries and much time spent in sickness, that I woke up to the idea that perhaps I was meant for better things, and my healing began.

Spirituality plays a significant role in my healing and also in achieving a life that is well beyond the reach of anorexia today. I literally reconstructed my thinking from feeling totally unsafe and fearful to feeling totally safe and living courageously. I came to understand that the only thing that mattered was my own opinions about myself. When they got better, so did I.

Fast forward to this moment... I still tend to be underweight, and some might describe me as skinny. The truth is I weigh more than I ever have before. My doctor says my weight and health are excellent, and I eat well. I workout regularly; I have more muscle and am in better shape now than when I was younger. I haven't had a scale in my home for at least a decade and I pay attention to how I'm feeling every day. I am an avid student of personal development and spiritual growth, and I live by what I have learned to be true, which we have now written in this book you are about to explore.

Today I live my dreams and I deserve to – so do you!

May every blessing find you every day. Thanks for being who you are.

Contact Information

To contact Deborah and/or Miranda personally please log on to:

http://www.just-say-yes-international.com and go to **"Contact Us"**

Call: **800 345 9688 Extension 0333**

Direct: **615 376 9905 (Nashville TN)**

Services offered individually include: Life Coaching, Fluent Sessions, Energy Work and more.

Also offered: Workshops / Tele-Seminars / Webinars and Speaking for groups, corporations and special events etc.
Life Coaching certification in the "**YES Method**".

Check out our Positive Media and Entertainment including: Music, CDs, Books, DVDs, the "**Just Say YES**" Show, the "**YES Fests**" Comedy, Documentaries and all aspects of media "in development now"!

Additional Journal Pages

Breinigsville, PA USA
04 September 2009
223512BV00002B/6/P

9 780972 045575